JAPAN INSCAPE

日本の心象風景

Michael A. Goldfarb M.D.

Published 2018 by WC Publishing

Printed in the United States of America

LCCN: 2018957562

WC Publishing
4625 Cedar Ford Blvd., Hastings, FL 32145
www.OnTargetWords.com/WCPublish
01-386-546-5164

WC Publishing is a division of On-Target Words

WC Publishing
an On-Target Words company
Hastings, Florida

DEDICATION

JAPAN INSCAPE is dedicated to my wife, Barbara. For more than 50 years we have shared a beautiful, rewarding, and poignant journey. My years in surgery presented challenges that only a smart and understanding partner could manage. As we near a new chapter, the joy of writing offers new trials. Barbara's love, guidance, and support were formative and intrinsic to my life experiences.

Glimpsed her high cheek bones.

Beauty has remained intact.

Look through gauze of years.

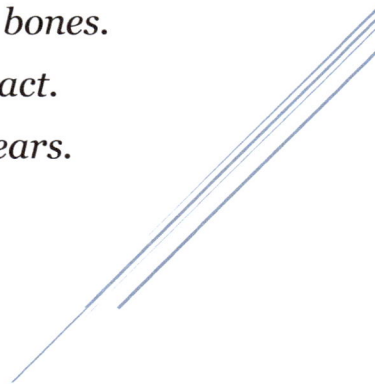

ACKNOWLEDGEMENTS

This book is a "thank you" to the people we met and the majestic and magical visions we saw during our time in Japan.

The sites photographed were, Kyoto area: Gion, Kabune, Ryoanji Temple, Sagano, Kinkauku-ji Temple, Takeo Ryokan, Nijo Castle, Kinkaku-ji Temple, and then: Miyajima Island, Hiroshima, Nara, Kanazawa, Takayama, Mt. Fuji, Hakone and Tokyo. The people were gracious and understanding. My impressions of historical and contemporary Japan are expressed through my poems and photographs. Not all of the photographs in this book are in sequence in relation to the above itinerary.

My wife, Barbara, shared the trip and sharpened my thinking each day. She spent countless hours helping me sort photographs and poems.

Toko Sakane, my neighbor in New Jersey for over 20 years, toured Kyoto with us. She showed us many enchanted sites that are documented in this book. Her incites were key to the quality of our visit. I have continued to discuss many moments with her since our return.

Nancy Quatrano provided the reality part of publishing a book, including manuscript and marketing consultation, cover and interior book layout and design, printing, publishing, and eBook formats. Her instant friendship and guidance made the process a positive experience that I will repeat.

PREFACE

Dark, light, dark, light, dark.
Leaves, plants, lilies, water, trees.
Nature alternates.

So does the Japan journey that I have called, *Japan Inscape*; an emotional response to an entire life of surgery and family, surfaced through poetry and photography.

The moment to write—
Launched by a leaf floating down,
Or news of a bomb

The mood alternates between chaotic city spaces and tranquil countryside, commonplace and monumental. Through this book I hope to inspire the reader to visit Japan and experience similar aesthetic highlights and discover many I have not yet enjoyed. The delight of coupling a Haiku poem to a photograph or a photograph to a poem, pressed me to continue to select and edit. The endpoint of a book forces final edits, and inevitable regrets. Only another visit can soothe those feelings.

Writing poems flow,
Like a stream not heard before.
And becomes a friend.

Where does it come from?
Energy unsuspected.
Truths—fountains of youth.

New poems more sound?
Is there greater clarity?
It's a lot of fun.

Water sheds flashbacks.
Swimming strokes raise old visions.
Friends return again.

Try to remember–
Haiku clear, as sleep covers.
But only note clouds.

Searching short poems,
Evolve from brain to fingers.
So easy, so hard.

Will sort through hundreds,
To find those that will linger.
Hard to predict best.

Inspired to have group-
Create verse and drink sake.
Ancient formula.

Word images lilt.
Voice flavors phrases' intent.
Wish music would blend.

Poems from photos.
Verses' chimes heard by reading.
Do we need photos?

Gion Geisha ghost—
Shuffles past half-moon window.
Focus reveals leaves.

Kyoto's dawn framed—
By mountain's squeezed, carved blue hues.
Await amazements.

Elegantly pure,
Art on hotel window sills.
Flowers, leaves, kiss lens.

Imagine Gion—
Full of Geisha and their men.
Still happens today.

Clean tiny dwellings,
Wait for crowds in train stations.
Opposites attract.

Neighbor knows store's gems,
We will share sake with her.
Poured from dark luster.

Garden plan revealed–
Perceptions change with each breath.
Intense view from edge.

First impression glance—
Not as deep as years of views—
But never relived.

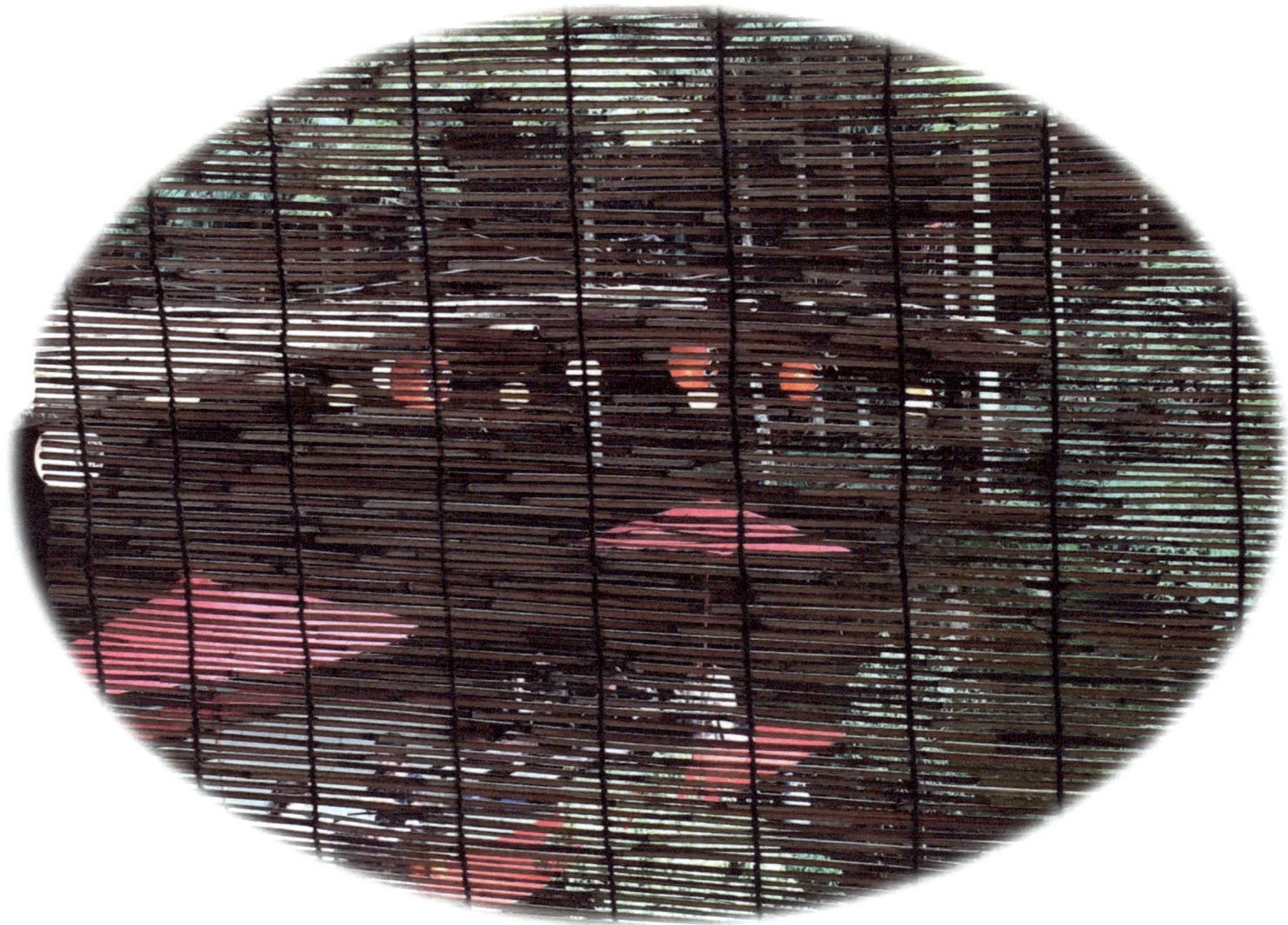

Wait to get seated.
To eat noodles sluicing down,
We lifted packets.

Cold, wet, light, white, batch–
Down bamboo paths, tugged out fast.
Until red noodles.

Tea cup age cherished.
Serving ritual witnessed,
Magic illusion.

Furious colors–
Head bobs, hands jab, feet stomp, dance.
Crowd afraid – but smirks.

Garden Rocks bounce back–
Monks energy from their minds.
To quiet, stunned, stares.

Streaked skin border hues.
Three walled sand-rock, Garden.
One wall is viewers.

Behold the vision.
Trees around garden flourish.
Swept sand, replaced trees.

Gift today to all,
Only way to be grateful now—
Write lines—sleep later.

Glimpsed trees, walls, sand, rocks.
But shimmers pulse hours later—
On mind screen in bed.

Shared for fifty years.
Love, children, home, surgery.
Cyclic water scenes.

Bamboo forest climbs—
Spiked plants grow as pattern.
Trust rickshaw driver.

Pure combinations,
Wood, leaf, green/white melded food—
Nicked tofu mishap.

Chance art created—
Started intact – food scraps dropped.
Sticks, chips and soy sauce.

Stark rice and spices
Cling to black bowl and sunshine.
Form and taste consumed.

We smile at stranger,
Did not know that our posed grins—
Grew larger later.

Tree sticks into clouds,
And sky is startled but calm.
First time both discerned.

Patterns of nature.
Fibonacci made big waves.
Started with rabbits.

All views are perfect.
Green fractals of moss gardens—
Tattooed on cortex.

Garden and water.
Old tree limb is supported.
Hope for destiny.

Dark, light, dark, light, dark.
Leaves, plants, lilies, water, trees.
Nature alternates.

Bridge calls over stream,
From one scene to the unseen.
Each step sounds a creak.

Warm walls and ceiling–
Surround guests in hallowed room.
Easy to recall.

Ice under salmon.
Lapis colored under-plate.
Food is more than taste.

Can frosted grapes cry?
Nurtured and traveled so far.
Savored by tourists.

Young Maiko white face,
Dances for us and time stops.
Top lip will get red.

Floors' nightingales chirp.
Palace guards know intruders,
By cadence of chirps.

Nails reveal secret.
Squeaking underside of floors,
Alarms palace guards.

Gilded palace watch—
Reflected gardens below.
Giant bonsai show.

Rolling landscape loved,
By travelers over bridge.
Awesome ride moment.

Piled sake cases.
Paired labels reveal secret.
Empty or to drink?

Water lilies wait—
For rain drops to kiss all leaves.
So sole can watch them.

Branches too fragile.
Wood crutches vertical lift.
Rocks arranged by chance?

Building punctures scene.
Hints glories below in streets—
And suffering times.

Sand is water waves?
Precise circles swept daily.
So many meanings.

Reflections with koi,
Tails blend ripples, trees prick heads.
Image hugs artists.

Fight the current or–
Flow with the river–choices.
Watch two koi swimming.

Strange, still, stealth, shapes, shades–
Workers clumps of protection.
Facing cool, dark kiln.

Doorway leads into—
Courtyard with poster missives.
Cannot decipher.

Revisit Gion.
Day displays dreary bright light.
Sky, walls, river, trees.

Crane walks on water.
Steps hidden by reflections.
Not a miracle.

Orchids celebrate–
New store opening custom.
Owner must feel pleased.

Mountains slowly watch—
Oyster beds sleep in sea waves.
And boats passing by.

Wall guides strollers to—
New surprises—old relics.
Road back is certain.

Miyajima deer—
Part of family portrait.
Next group waits in line.

Tourists get tickets.
Man's best friend will also tour.
But not in this group.

Lanterns line both sides.
Colors, design, and drizzle–
Art dictates function.

Gold and green Lanterns,
Orange pillars, brown borders.
Echoes along light.

Grilled oysters, just so.
Miss shell's morsel savored then.
Specie, recipe?

Stone's hole, a round frame—
Highlights wading, orange, shrine.
Spot now glued in mind.

Sika deer for her–
To pet and feed and revere.
Animal lover.

Stark Shinto shrine wades–
Water full of clinging crabs.
Both are same color.

All eyes feel comfort–
From Golden Mean Measurements.
Search Wabi-Sabi.

Bombed building's last bricks—
Left as reminder shocker.
Streets are rubbish free.

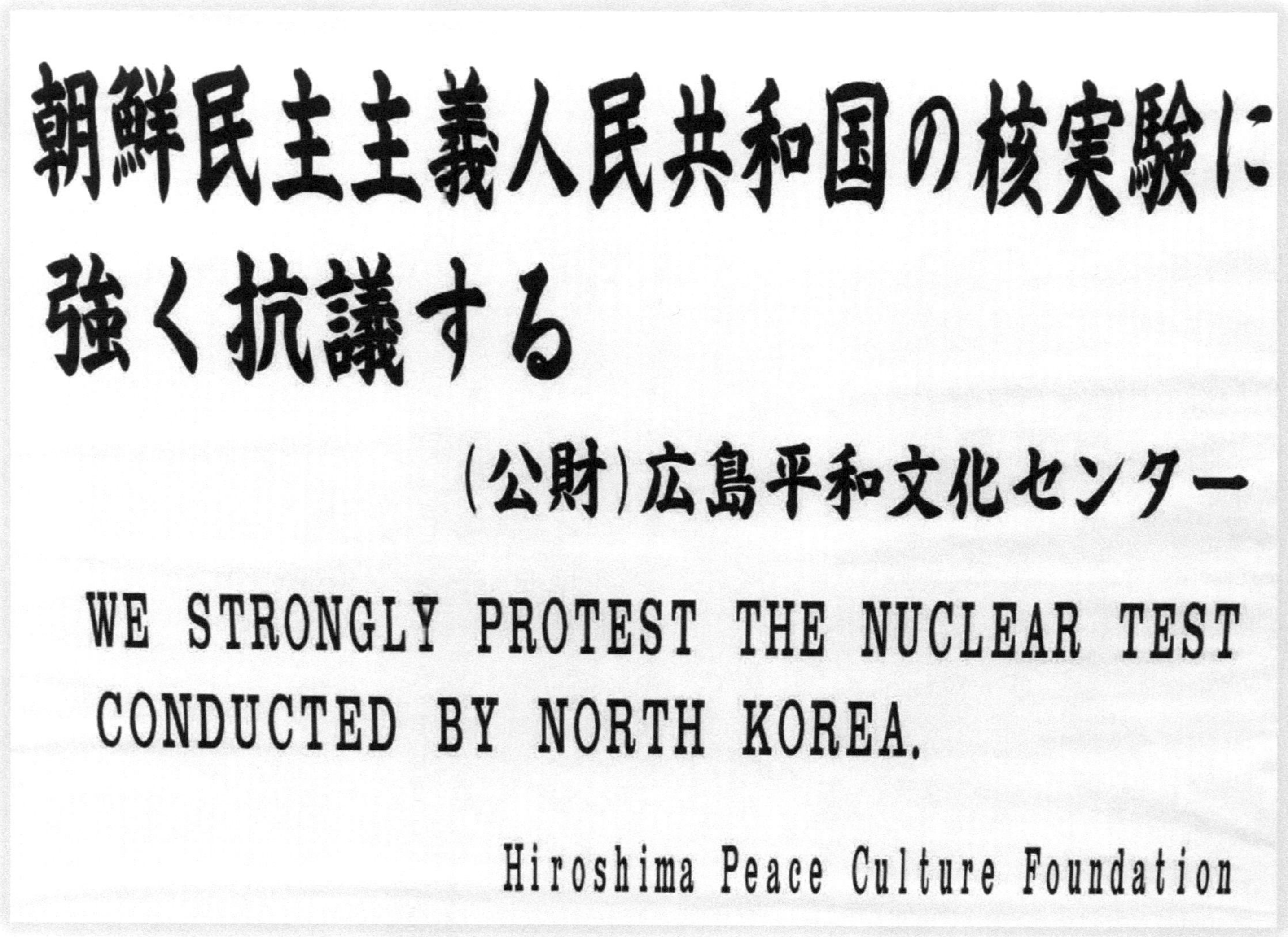

朝鮮民主主義人民共和国の核実験に
強く抗議する

（公財）広島平和文化センター

WE STRONGLY PROTEST THE NUCLEAR TEST
CONDUCTED BY NORTH KOREA.

Hiroshima Peace Culture Foundation

Sign at exhibit.
Must never happen again.
Hiroshima proof.

Poured clouds embrace trees.
Paint blue, white, and green near lens.
So much still to see.

Follow wind in trees.
Large branches shake to one side.
While twig ends flutter.

Read about culture.
But touching now is profound.
Wabi-Sabi hints.

Prayer and incense—
Devotees shop, eat, inhale.
Lines, throw coins in bin.

Fresh dough meant to eat.
Gilded bread for sale.
Not seen in Brooklyn.

Cocoon cages wait.
Opened by women spinners.
Hundred spun per tie.

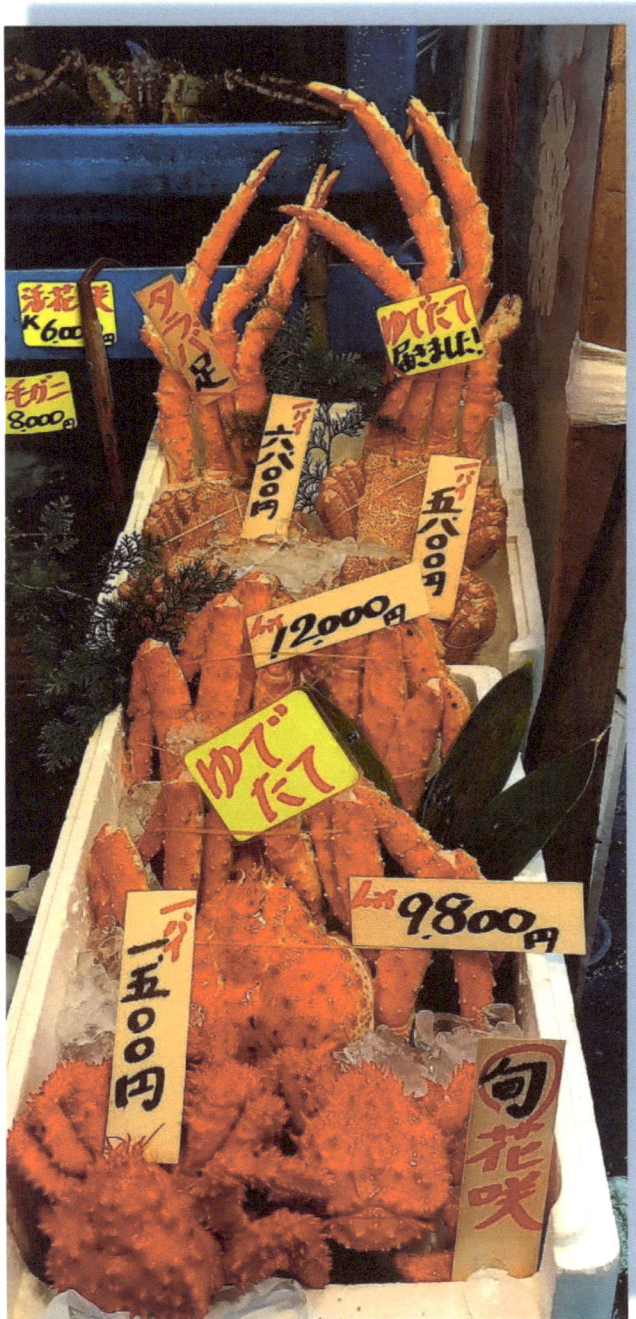

First remove price tags.
Close spaces—make cylinders.
Shinto deep pillars.

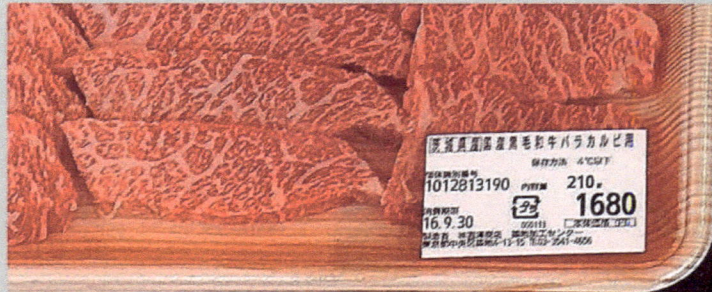

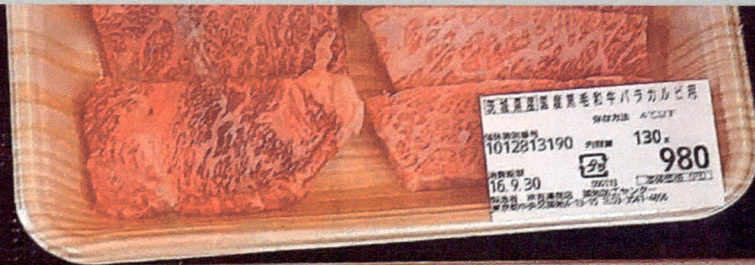

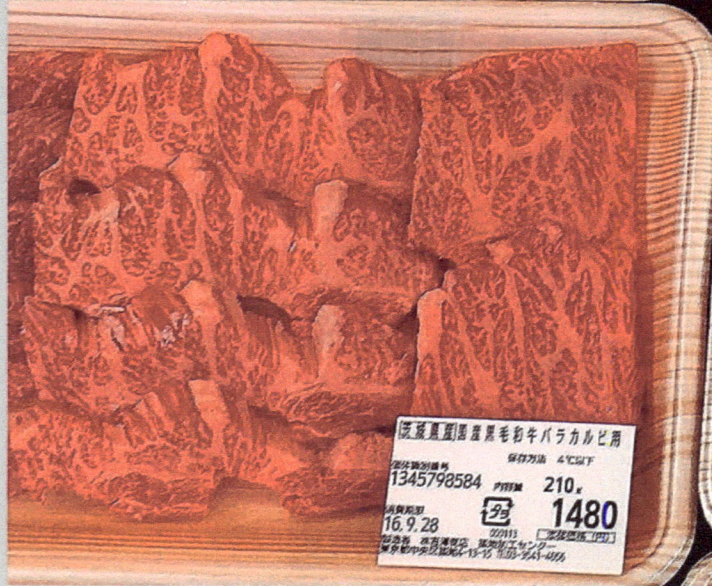

Four share Wagyu lunch.
Longing dreams of dreamy taste.
Ever know again?

Tokyo streets stream–
Godzilla has protected.
City pride–no trash.

Whispers of cloud winds—
Weave mountains, waters, dwellings.
Now indelible.

Food great—view improved.
Glimpse—photo—photo—swallow.
Her date—a surprise.

Train station mid-day.
No wasted space or space waste.
Spotless culture rules.

Tokyo shared view,
High perch—crisp, busy, clean streets,
Calm crowds, not discerned.

Plane will soon touch down.
Flight complete with jet lag week.
But Japan–intense.

Dog will see us soon–
Never knows where, or time gone.
Barks very happy.

Abstract nature's gems–
Strengthens resolve to create,
And deal with evil.

Eastern ways now shine.
Studied just Western courses.
Now lived, more truth forms.

Will sort through hundreds,
To find those that will linger.
Hard to predict best.

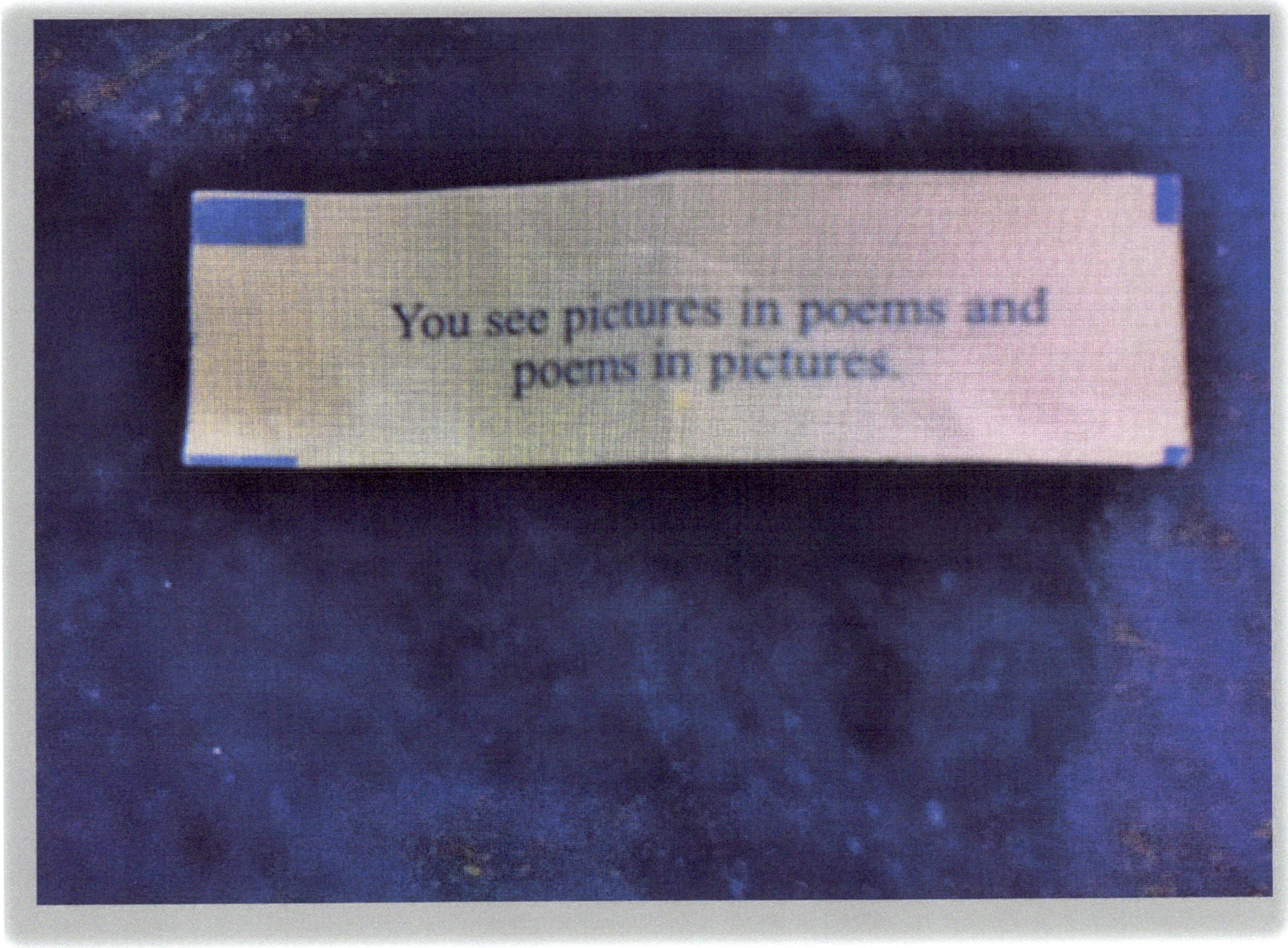
You see pictures in poems and
poems in pictures.

ABOUT THE AUTHOR

Dr. Goldfarb, a surgeon for over forty years, loves his family, his dogs and the many riverside birds he sees every day. He is a teacher of surgery and avid student and stresses the beauty of surgical procedures and patient outcomes.

After a reflective trip to Japan in 2016, he wrote, *Japan Inscape*, which includes photographs and Haiku about historic and modern Japan. He has written Haiku for many years. The journey and respect of the search for the "way" is shared by some poems explained by photos, and some photos explained by poems.

www.ingramcontent.com/pod-product-compliance
Lightning Source LLC
Chambersburg PA
CBHW040710150426

42811CB00061B/1809